Mommy and Wee Travels LLC Presents:

BOOK 1

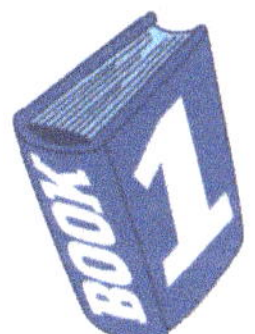

Let's Explore Paris with Isabella

Written By
Isabella Cooley

Illustrated By
Whimsical Designs by CJ

I would like to thank God for watching over us. I would like to thank my mommy Tyra for loving, encouraging and caring for me. Thank you to my daddy Robert for being there for me. I would like to thank my baby cousin Tory for being my biggest playmate and I want to thank my bigger cousins Nyjhia for being a good role model and my cousins Tavoris and Deamonta for teaching me how to stand up for myself. I also want to thank my aunts Andrisha and Shantelle for caring and loving me like a daughter.

Lastly, I would like to thank all of my other family members and friends for being some of my biggest supporters. You guys rock!

Thank you

Isabella Cooley

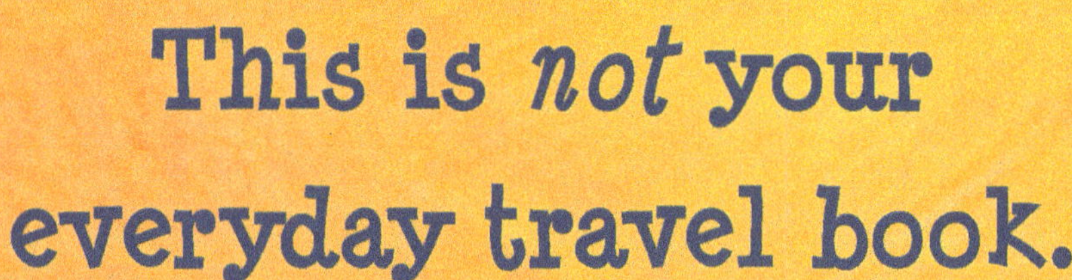

This book will teach you amazing facts about Paris while taking you on a journey with us. We are going to learn how to say words in a different language and we are going to use our imagination to visualize Paris. You will notice that all of the words that we will be learning will be colored in red.

BONUS:

At the end of this book, be on the lookout for your scavenger hunt coloring page as well as your word search puzzle to keep you busy while on your next vacation.

I'm Isabella Cooley and I'm your official Kid Fun Director of all things concerning travel! Come along on this journey with me, as we explore all of the beautiful, fun and tasty things of Paris with my mommy.
We are going to have a blast and eat delicious foods while we learn about the different cultural things of Paris.

Come on, it's time to board our airplane!

I'm traveling from Florida to Paris so this means that we will be flying in an airplane for about 9 hours at night so I will be sleeping on most of our airplane trip to Paris. Oh and this is my first time flying outside of the United States Of America for travel fun. I'm so excited. Did you know that flying on an airplane to a different country is called an international flight?

Since we are flying to a different country from the United States, it means that we will need our passports and it also means that we will be seeing and hearing many things in Paris that are different from what we are used to seeing and hearing back home.

Come on, let's explore those things now!

FUN FACT
Did you know that it is called a "Red Eye Flight" when you get onto an airplane at night and don't land at your destination until the next morning?

Bonjour again!

We have arrived in Paris! Bonjour means good morning and *hello* in French. French is the language that most people speak here in Paris but don't worry, many people also speak English in Paris like we do in the United States.

At the Paris Airport we will be looking for our driver **Pierre** who will have our names on a sign so that we can easily find him. Pierre will be our driver and tour guide for the entire time that we are in Paris.

Merci' Pierre, that's *thank you* in French. "Thanks so much for helping us with our bags and guiding us through Paris."

*** FUN Fact ***

Did you know that Paris is a city in France and France is the most visited country in the world?

After we have arrived and settled into our beautiful resort, off to the Carousel Of The Eiffel Tower we go! It sure wasn't fun unpacking our luggage at our resort but ooh la la I know that I'm going to have so much fun today.

The Carousel Of The Eiffel Tower is super famous because you can see the Eiffel Tower right behind it. This carousel is one of the best carousels that I have ever been on!

After my carousel ride, my mommy and I spent time just walking around enjoying all of the beautiful sights and smells of Paris. I can hear the carousel ride music, I can hear the birds chirping,

I can smell the desserts from the food stand and
I can see people taking pictures of the Eiffel Tower.

FUN FACT

Did you know that this is the only

carousel in Paris that goes clockwise?

Have you ever heard of The Louvre Museum?
It is the biggest and most visited museum in the
world! The main entrance to the Louvre Museum
looks like a pyramid that is built out of shiny
glass. It's called the Pyramide du Louvre
and it is about **69** feet tall!

Can you believe that it is taller than
3 giraffes standing on top of eachother???
That's huge!
Inside of the Louvre Museum, it is so pretty!
It looks just like a castle on the inside.

*** FUN FacT***

If you looked at every piece of artwork in

The Louvre Museum for 30 seconds,

it would take you 100 full days to visit them all.

My mommy has told me about the many amazing things that are here in the Louvre Museum, but the painting that I want to see the most is the Mona Lisa. She told me that this painting is one of the most expensive paintings in the entire world and that it was painted by an artist named Leonardo Da Vinci.

Look, we have found the Winged Victory (NIke) Sculpture. Oh Look there is the Venus de Milo Sculpture and wait is that the Mona Lisa? YES we found it too! It is smaller than I thought it would be but it still looks amazing. Oh, did we have a blast at the museum.

*** FUN FaCt ***

The Mona Lisa was estimated to be worth almost $1 Billion. That's almost enough to buy all of the Disney World Parks and property in Orlando, Florida.

MONA LISA
VENUS DE MILO
Nike
15

DISNEY LAND
16

Did you know that there was also a Disney Land In Paris? Two of my favorite rides at Disney of all time are the " Big Thunder Mountain and the Toy Story Ride". We will be going really really fast on Big Thunder Mountain so hold on to your glasses and hats.
Are You ready?

Lets go!

Ahhhhhhhhhhhhhhhhhhhh.

What rides do you like to ride at Disney?
What do you like to eat when you are at Disney?
My favorite thing to eat at
Disney is the ice cream!

Yum-Yum

FUN Fact

Did you know that there are

12 Disney Parks across the world?

Have You Ever Had A Picnic in a cool park before?
I think that the best park for a picnic in Paris is
the Champs de Mars Park and yep you got it, this
is exactly where we had a picnic at. This park
gives you a perfect view of the Eiffel Tower while
you are eating your lunch.

Our picnic was made up of yummy fruits, French cheeses, fresh lunch meats, a tasty apple tart and the best French bread ever. All of our lunch was laid out perfectly on our Paris picnic blanket. At the Champs de Mars Park I also made a new friend, her name was Claire and we played until we were sooo very tired. While we were playing she taught me how to count to 10 in French!

Count with me!

*** FUN FACT ***

Count To 10
In French With Me

0. zéro (zeh-ro)
1. un (uh)
2. deux (duh)
3. trois (twah)
4. quatre (kat-ruh)
5. cinq (sank)
6. six (sees)
7. sept (set)
8. huit (weet)
9. neuf (nuhf)
10. dix (dees)

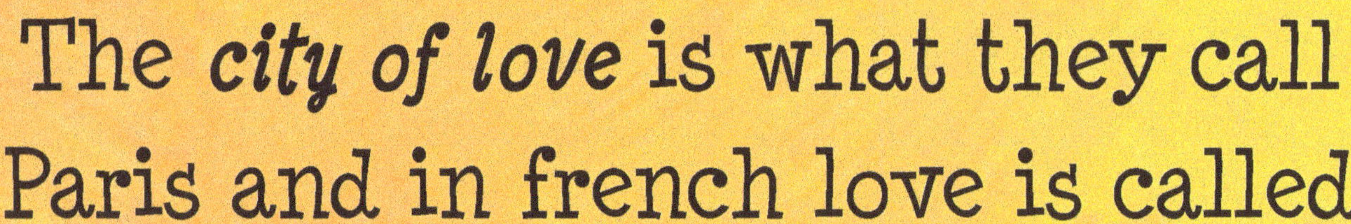

The *city of love* is what they call Paris and in french love is called l'amour.

Let's pronounce it together " (la mooore)". In Paris,my mommy and I spent one day expressing our love for ourselves and each other. We started our day with a bunch of hugs and kisses, wayyy too many mommy kisses if you would ask me but my mommies hugs and kisses are the best. We then put on our matching red dresses and we were off to our love filled day.

Our breakfast was really fancy and I even got a chance to taste real french croissants and a chocolate filled pastry called a "Pain au chocolat" for the first time. The chocolate pastry was so good but the croissant was the best that I have ever had because it melted in my mouth.

What's your favorite breakfast food?

After breakfast, we did so many special things in Paris on that day. Our last stop was at the "Love Lock Bridge".

At this bridge we were able to see so many locks.
These locks are a symbol to express love for
yourself or someone else. Once the lock is placed
on the bridge, it is locked and the key is tossed into
a river called the Seine River. Tossing the key into
the river expresses a never ending love for someone
or yourself.

So that's just what we did!
Let's throw the key into the river.
We threw our keys very far into the river.

The biggest symbol of love in Paris is the Eiffel Tower and it is really really big. There are three different floors to visit there but we are only going to go on an adventure to the first and second floors. Up on the elevator we go

WEEEEeeeee!.

Let's walk around the entire first floor and explore it. It's so cool we can see the entire city from up here! On the first floor I see and hear a lot of kids playing and learning about the Eiffel Tower. Ok now it's time for us to learn!

Do you think that the Eiffel Tower is the tallest thing in Paris? Did you say yes or no? If you said yes then you are right. Yes, the Eiffel Tower is the tallest thing standing in Paris!

Now onto the second floor. On this floor we were able to get some lunch. I ate a yummy french sandwich with a few colorful Paris treats that I have never tried before. They were called Macarons and each color dessert had a different flavor.

On the second floor of the Eiffel Tower, things looked even smaller. I can even see the Louvre Museum and the Seine River from here.

Oh what a great day that this was! I will never forget this love filled day.

*** FUN Fact***

The Eiffel Tower is 1,063 feet tall! That is taller than 30 school buses standing up, directly on top of each other.

As our Paris trip comes to an end, let's go on a Paris City Bus Tour. On the tour bus, we sat at the very top of the bus so that we could see everything. Our first stop was at Sainte-Chapelle Chapel and if you like pretty colors, you will love seeing the beautiful windows of this royal chapel. We also saw the Notre Dame Cathedral, but we couldn't go inside because it was being repaired from a recent fire at the church.

We stopped at a few places but our last fun stop was at the Arc De Triomphe. We got there in enough time to see the Eternal Flame Ceremony that happens every day at 630pm. During this ceremony, military veterans honor the unknown soldier that died during the Great War and they keep the eternal flame burning all night.

*** FUN Fact ***

The Eternal flame at the Arc de Triomphe monument has been burning since 1923. That's nearly **100** years that this flame has been burning. It has been burning even before the first man walked on the moon. Wow

ARC DE TRIOMPHE
SAINTE-CHAPELLE CHAPEL

Thank you so much for coming on this Paris explorer trip with my family.Paris was amazing and I can't wait to come back. If you have extra time in Paris you should also check out the Palace Of Versailles. It is really fun and it is just a train ride away from Paris. I hope that I have inspired you to read about other adventures and I can't wait to see all of your vacation pictures including Paris.

Don't forget to have your parents tag us on your next vacation pictures so that we can explore the world together or maybe we can meet up for a group trip someday. This would be awesome!

Also make sure to take this book with you when you visit Paris to check off everything that you have done. Lastly, don't forget to use your Paris coloring page and word search puzzle while flying to and from Paris or your next vacation.

Explorers whenever you come to Paris, use this scavenger hunt as a checklist for fantastic places that you should try to visit.

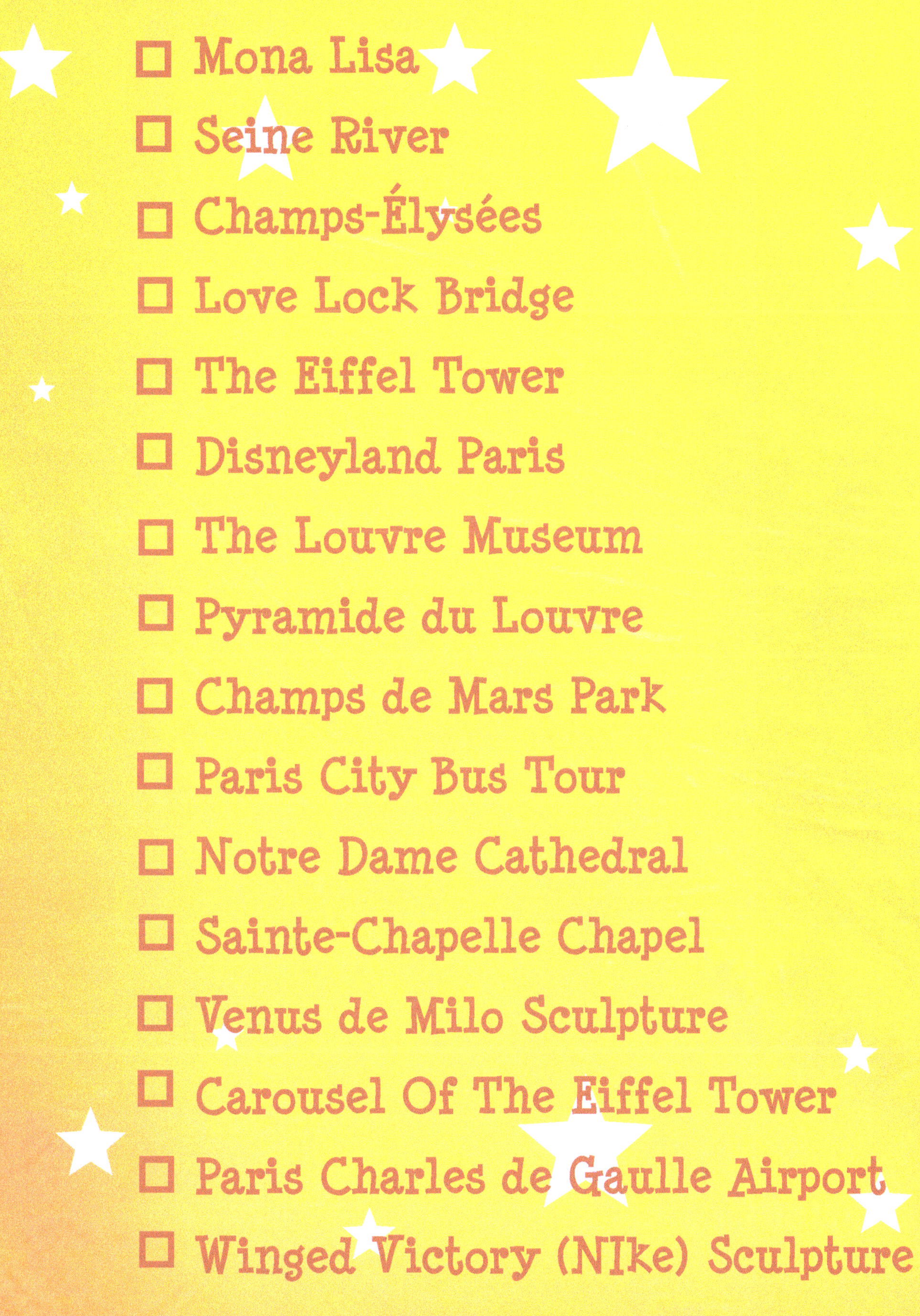

☐ Mona Lisa
☐ Seine River
☐ Champs-Élysées
☐ Love Lock Bridge
☐ The Eiffel Tower
☐ Disneyland Paris
☐ The Louvre Museum
☐ Pyramide du Louvre
☐ Champs de Mars Park
☐ Paris City Bus Tour
☐ Notre Dame Cathedral
☐ Sainte-Chapelle Chapel
☐ Venus de Milo Sculpture
☐ Carousel Of The Eiffel Tower
☐ Paris Charles de Gaulle Airport
☐ Winged Victory (NIke) Sculpture

Thanks For
Exploring
Paris
With Me

Lets Explore Paris With Isabella

Word Search Puzzle

Paris

French

Isabella

Explorer

Louvre

Mona Lisa

Eiffel Tower

Versaille

Train

Love

Bonjour

WORD BANK: BONJOUR, EIFFELTOWER, EXPLORER, FRENCH, ISABELLA, LOUVRE, LOVE, MONALISA, PARIS, TRAIN, VERSAILLE

Name ________________________________

Let's Explore Paris With Isabella Workbook

1) What country is Paris located? _______!

2)What two languages are spoken in Paris? __________ & __________!

3) How do you say hello in French? ______ !

4) How do you write Number Three (3) In French? _________ !

5)How many school buses can fit the length of the Eiffel Tower? _________ !

6)Who painted the Mona Lisa? __________ !

7) How many floors does the Eiffel Tower have? __________ !

8) What is the most visited place in the world?_______ !

9) How many Disney parks are there? ______!

10) Which Cathedral in Paris was being fixed because of a fire? __________!